The Trump Dictionary, Volume 1

A Political Satire

Mainly in His Own Words

by

Ray Sweatman

ISBN: 978-1-387-30803-3

Author's Note:

The Dictionary is told from the point of view of Trump, chiefly in his own words.

Quotation marks denote direct or closely paraphrased quotes from Donald Trump--unless otherwise attributed.

Volume One covers Trump through early October of 2017, the first 300 words or so.

A

Accessories: Women. See **8-10 rating.** Women with moles need not apply.

Admission: Real men never admit they're wrong. And it helps when you're never wrong.

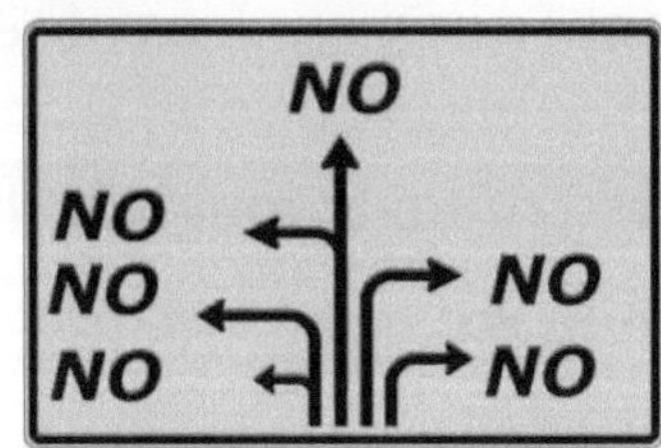

Alec Baldwin: 'Impersonation can't get any worse.'

Al Gore: A phoney who scams those who don't believe in scientific facts and retards the growth of great corporations.

Alternative Facts: Sexy, brilliant term invented by Kellyanne Conway. For those too dumb to understand, it means there is an alternative universe that exists in the minds of me the Donald and my followers. Non-believers and the enemy Media are too dopey and dishonest to see it. See **Bowling Green Massacre.** See **Swedish Terrorism.**

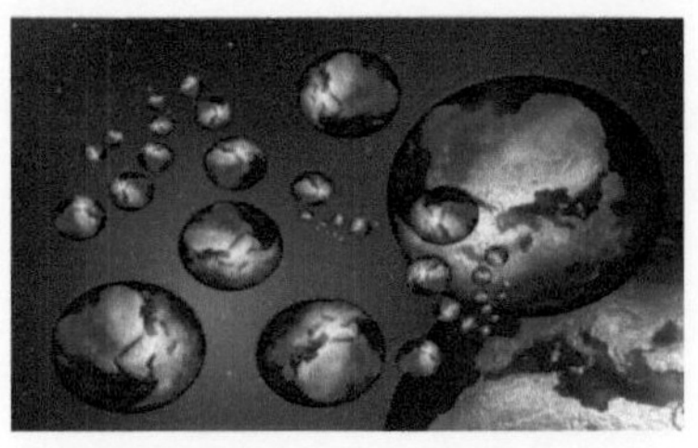

Alt-Right: Great people who want to make America great again. Don't See **Politically Correct Term for White Supremacist Hate Groups.** Only a moron would see that.

Amazon: 'A great damage to tax-paying retailers. Amazon doesn't pay taxes.' Don't See **Reality Check.** That's the dishonest dopey loser author of this book trying to mess with you.

America: The greatest country on earth until the slaves were freed and non-white folk started to immigrate here.

Anthony Scaramucci, Communications Director for Ten Days: What? You can't use colorful, politically incorrect words like suck, fuck, cock or cockblock these days? See **Political Correctness.**

Apologize: Real men don't say they're sorry. Ever.

Apprentice: 'All of the women on *The Apprentice* flirted with me – consciously or unconsciously. That's to be expected.'

Unconscious Woman Flirting with the Donald

Archie Bunker: A thousand times smarter than Meathead.

Ariana Huffington: 'She is unattractive, both inside and out. I fully understand why her former husband left her for a man – he made a good decision.'

Arnold Schwarzenegger: Even the great Arnold Schwartze-the 'N' word-couldn't replace me! Ratings for *The Apprentice* fell like Rosie O'Donnell trying to fly!

The Ratings Terminator

Arrogance: It's not arrogance. It's New York confidence.

You Want the Horns, Little Rocket Man?

Art of the Deal: Political Connections, Huge Tax Subsidies, Sue 'Til You Get It. See **How I Got 885 Million in Tax Breaks from New York City**

Welcome to the Grand Hyatt, Congressman.

Asbestos: '100 percent safe. I believe that the movement against asbestos was led by the mob, because it was often mob-related companies that would do the asbestos removal. Great pressure was put on politicians, and as usual, the politicians relented. Millions of truckloads of this incredible fire-proofing material were taken to special 'dump sites' and asbestos was replaced by materials that were supposedly safe but couldn't hold a candle to asbestos in limiting the ravages of fire.' See **Science.**

Australian Health Care System: 'Your healthcare is better than ours.' See **Wait! I Didn't Know It Includes Single-Payer**. I don't know what single-payer is, but I know it's a Curse on the American People.

B

Baldness: 'The worst thing a man can do is go bald. Never let yourself go bald.' See **Phalacrophobia.**

Baltimore Thugs: 'Our great African-American President hasn't exactly had a positive impact on the thugs who are so happily and openly destroying Baltimore.'

Barack Obama: 'He was such a bad president. It will be generations before we elect another African American.'

Barry Soetoro: 'Obama's real name.' See **It Ain't A Conspiracy If Me and My Fans Believe It's True**. See **Evidence.**

Base: The smartest and finest people in America, who love me dearly. See **Time to Kow-Tow-To Them Before Poll Approval Numbers Plummet to Zero.**

Beauty: 'The beauty of me is that I'm very rich.'

Bernie Sanders, Senator from Vermont: 'He could've been a legend, but he sold out to Hillary. He is turning out to be a weak and somewhat pathetic figure, wants it all to end!' Colonel Chicken Sanders. Bok Bok Bok!

Bill and Hillary Clinton Philanthropic Organization: 'Criminal Enterprise.'

Birtherism: 'Obama was not born in the United States.' See **The Power of the Mind to Believe What It Wants To.**

Black Accountants: 'Black guys counting my money! I hate it. The only kind of people I want counting my money are short guys wearing yarmulkes. Those are the only kind of people I want counting my money. Nobody else. Besides that, I tell you something else. I think that's guy's lazy. And it's probably not his fault because laziness is a trait in blacks,' John O'Donnell quoting Trump in his 1991 book, *Trumped! The Inside Story of the Real Donald Trump.*

See **I Said It Was Probably True in 1997 In A Playboy Interview And Then Denied Ever Saying It Two Years Later When Running for Reform Party's Nomination for President.**

Blonde Polish Reporter in the White House:

'You're lookin' fit.'

Bok-Bok-Bok: See **Bernie 'Colonel' Sanders.**

Boring and Overrated: Any show or entertainer who parodies or protests the Donald.

Bowling Green Massacre: Proof that we need extensive Travel Ban against Muslims! See **Imaginary Events.** See **Kellyanne Conway.**

Breaking Bad: See **Fake News.**

Breitbart: Alt-Right website masterminded by former Strategic Adviser, Steve Bannon. See **Almost As Smart As the Donald.**

Breastfeeding Lawyers: 'Disgusting.' Don't See **Barney Frank's Protruding Nipples.**

Brigitte Macron, French First Lady: 'You're in such great shape.'

How Do you Say *Swing* in French?

Brilliant: Putin's astute assessment of my big, big brain.

Britain: 'Trying hard to disguise their massive Muslim problem.'

Bullying: Twitter is the greatest tool of the 20th century. See **Twitter.**

It makes me feel so good to hit "sleazebags" back -- much better than seeing a psychiatris (which I never have!)

See **Self-Awareness.**

C

The Cabinet: Don't see **Musical Chairs.**

Call from Boy Scout Leadership: 'I got a call from the head of the Boy Scouts saying it was the greatest speech that was ever made to them, and they were very thankful.' Don't See **Nope, Never Happened from Boy Scout Head.** Instead See **Because I'm Your Commander-in-Chief and I Say So.**

Call from Enrique Pena Nieto's, President of Mexico: 'Even the President of Mexico called me. Their southern border, they said very few people are coming because they know they're not going to get to our border, which is the ultimate compliment.' See **Just 'Cause He Doesn't Remember It, Doesn't Make it Untrue.**

Too Many Tequila Worms?

Carmen Yulin Cruz, Mayor San Juan Puerto Rico: 'Such poor leadership ability by the Mayor of San Juan, and others in Puerto Rico, who are not able to get their workers to help. They want everything to be done for them when it should be a community effort. 10,000 Federal workers now on Island doing a fantastic job.'

'Politically Motivated Ingrates.'

Central Park Five: Yeah, I took out 85,000 dollars worth of ads in the papers and called for the Death Penalty before the trial had even started against five black and latino teenagers accused of rape in Central Park in 1989. D-N-A SCHEE-N-A! I don't care what the D-N-A SCHEE-N-A testing said years later. I don't believe it. 'They should've gotten the death penalty. These young men do not have the past of angels.'

Chapter 11: 'Stop saying I went bankrupt. I never went bankrupt but like many great business people have used the laws to corporate advantage—smart!'

See **Smart Business Bankruptcies: Trump Taj Mahal 1991, Trump Castle 1992, Trump Plaza and Casino 1992, Plaza Hotel 1992, Trump Hotels and Casinos Resorts 2004, Trump Entertainment Resorts, 2009.**

Bankruptcy is good, Dopey!

Cher: 'No, it's not a rug...and I promise not to talk about your massive plastic surgeries that didn't work.'

C.I.A.: 'Disgraceful, politically motivated, sick people.'

Civil Rights Laws: The next thing you know, they'll have us paying reparations and splitting our property with them. See **A Leftist Plot to Instill Political Correctness**.

Collusion: Schma-Lusion. My friends love me so much. They do things without me asking them to. See **Russians**.

Columbia University: 'Obama never attended Columbia University and if he did he was a bad student. I offered 50 thousand dollars to charity for Obama to release his school records. He ignored me. Hackers please find out the truth.' See **It Ain't Delusional If Me and My Fans Believe It.**

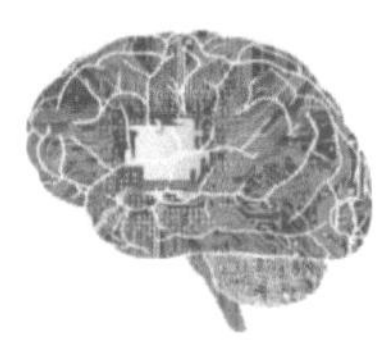

Confederate Generals: 'The same as Washington and Jefferson. You want to take their statues too?'

We'd rather die than be a part of the USA! We are the CSA!

Confederate Statues: Monuments to great men, who fought like the dickens to keep this country great.

I wish I was in Dixie. You have to admit we had better songs.

Conflation: Don't know what that means, but I'm sure it was caused by Democrats.

Congress: A dysfunctional set of misfits who'd never make it in the real world.

Couch Potatoes for Trump: Conserving our finite energy. Living longer. See **Exercise**.

My belly hurts. Have you seen the remote?

Covfefe: The passcode to nuclear weapons. See **Russian intelligence.** See **My Cutest Tweet To Date.**

Crooked Hillary: 'Don't let this golf ball hit you on the way out, you crooked bigot! Yeah, all you see is people of color... and your buddy Obama and Bill, too...It's because of you the country is in the state that it's in!'

Take this Presidential Swing!

Curse on the American People: Single-Payer Health System, Universal Care for Everyone.

D

Death Penalty: What strong country doesn't have one?

Death Threats to Those Who Disagree: Loyal Base. Good boys. I always wanted a Pit Bull.

Democracy: Democracy's great. We live in the greatest country on earth. It's just all its institutions I can't stand--the moronic separation of powers, the dumb Congress, the dumber intelligence agencies, the dumbest judiciary branch and the dumberest of all, the fake news press. I bet Putin never had to deal with this!

Democrats: 'Their total weakness is the greatest recruiting tool for ISIS.' Donkeys with their heads up their incompetent asses.

Dictator: Now, that's the life. They got it made in the shade. See **Democracy.**

Disabled Reporter: When the enemy asks a stupid question, they deserve to be mocked.

Disaster: See **Obamacare.** Don't See **Hurricane Maria in Puerto Rico. They were already messed up.**

Discriminatory Housing Law Suit, 1973: 'We weren't racist, just choosy.' What right do they have to tell us how to run our own business? Yeah, we settled out of court. Peanuts to us. Just the government flexin' its left-wing, authoritarian muscles.

Who Chose the Black Pencil? Fired!

Disgusting: 'Heather Heyer, Obama Administration, Crooked Hillary, New York Times, CNN, Media, Fox News (except My Main Man, Hannity), Breastfeeders, Marco Rubio, Mayor Nutter of Philadelphia, Mexican Court System, Kenya Moore, Saturday Night Live, Windmill at Royal Aberdeen, Iowa Wind Farms, Barney Frank's Nipples…'

Dishonest: Any one who criticizes me, especially members of the Free Press.

Divisive: See the **Free Press** and **the Loser Protesters.**

DNA: Schnee N A. See **Science.**

The Donald: The Greatest President Ever. Restoring American Greatness In My Own Godly Image. Smarter than Science. Richer Than You. Sexier Than You. See **The Big, Nay, Huuuuuuge Rocket Man.**

Dopey: See 'Mark Cuban, Robert Gates, Maureen Dowd, Tony Schwarz, Bill Kristol, Paul Begala, Mort Zuckerman, Mitt Romney, Karl Rove, Brit Hume, Charles Krauthammer, Frank Bruni, Chris Stirewalt, Charles Lane, Harry Hurt, Lawrence O'Donnell, Jon Stewart, Barack Obama, Dr. Thomas Frieden, Graydon Carter, Bryant Gumbel, Ariana Huffington, The Author of This Book...' See **Dumb.**

Drama: Good for ratings.

Dreams of My Father: 'Masterpiece written by Bill Ayers not Obama.' Obama couldn't have written that book. He's Afr--Bla-- He's Obama, for Chrissakes. See **Windmills as Evil Giants.**

Dumb: Anyone who disagrees or has the balls to criticize me.

Dumbo the Elephant: The Republican Establishment.

E

Ebola's Great Gift: 'Something very important, and indeed society changing, may come out of the Ebola epidemic that will be a very good thing: No Shaking Hands!' See **Germs.**

Echangistes: *Swingers* in French. See **You're in Great Shape.**

Eclipse: Real men don't need sunglasses even during an eclipse. See **Stupid Scientists.** See **If You Can Tell Two Blonde Finnish Reporters Apart After Trying This.**

Bring it on, Sun!

Education: Another Liberal tool to instill Political Correctness. You can learn more on the street and Twitter.

No, Arnold, it's B for Bat.

Edward Snowden: 'Traitor. See **Death Penalty.**'

Egotistical: See **Narcissism.**

I am such a fox.

The Einstein of Gaining Political Power Via The Lowest Common Denominator: See **Steve Bannon.**

Election of 2016: 'Rigged by the dishonest media!' See **Well, That's What I Thought When I Was Losing.**

Elephant in the Room: See **Republicans.**

Elizabeth Warren, Senator from Massachusetts: 'Pocahantas. Goofy. She made up her heritage, which I think is racist. I think she's a racist, actually because what she did was very racist. Total Fraud.'

The Enemy: The Mainstream Media. Certainly not Putin. That dude is cooler than Megyn Kelly's...See **Wink.**

Enrique Pena Nieto's, President of Mexico: See **Having Lunch Behind the Wall, Paying A Small Fee to Enjoy the View.**

No Graffiti, please.

Equal Rights: See **Civil Rights Laws.**

Evangelicals:

'We did well with the Evangelicals,' the Donald says, speaking to two pastors.
'We're mainstream Presbyterians not Evangelicals.'
'Well, you're Christian, aren't you?'
'Yes. Aren't you?'
'Yes. Presbyterian. We did well with the Evangelicals.'

Evolution: Nah. Don't believe in it. I believe in De-evolution. See **Make America Great Again.**

Everyone is Created Equal: Of course. Everyone knows that. Don't see **Wink.**

Evidence: Who needs evidence when you have belief--unless you're coming after me, then see low-life lawyers on a **Witch Hunt.**

Exercise: 'A person is like a battery born with a finite amount of energy. Exercise will make you die sooner.'

A Man After My Own Heart--Lazy Cows for Trump

F

Factual: See **Evidence**.

Failin': All media outlets that are jealous of the Donald's success.

Fake News: Any bit of factual information that shows me in a negative light.

Smashing the First Amendment One Outlet at a Time

Feminism: Created by a woman too ugly to qualify for Miss Universe.

Fingers: 'My fingers are long and beautiful, as, it has been well documented, are various other parts of my body.'

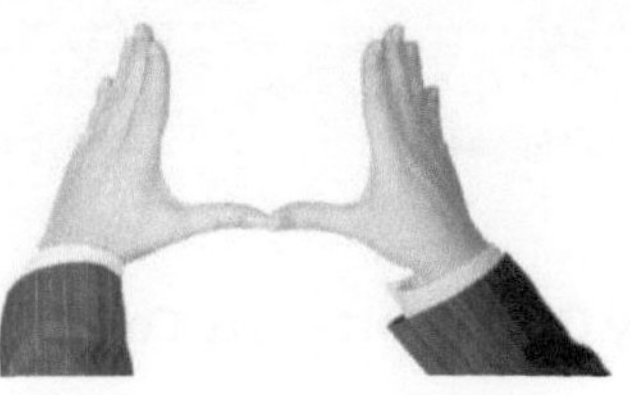

Real News

Finland and Russia: 'Russia and Finland have gotten along for a hundred years. Because you both like blonde women.' Don't see **Reality Check.** See instead **How Can You Be Doomed to Repeat What You Never Did Or Knew Of in the First Place.**

Fired!: See the Wrath of the Donald, a never-ending display of power and potency, potent power, powerful potency, very very potent; great for the ratings.

Five Military Draft Deferments: What's the purpose of being rich if you can't have privileges? At least I didn't lie about my military record like Blumenthal!

The Flag: You must stand up and salute out of respect. A large likeness of me will also do. Or the Confederate Flag. See **Base**.

That works, too.

Flatchested Women: 'It's hard for a flatchested woman to be a 10.'

Former Miss Universe, Alicia Machado: 'Miss Piggy. A Real Problem.' See **Eating Machine.**

Former National Security Advisor, Michael Flynn: Good guy, no need to investigate his Russian dealings. See **Comey, Fired.**

Former Swedish Prime Minister Carl Bildt: 'Sweden? Terror attack? What has he been smoking? Questions abound,' Bildt. See **Swedish Terrorist Attack.**

Fred Trump, Father, Arrested at KKK Rally, 1926: What apple? What tree?

Free Press: The enemy of a great country.

G

General John Pershing: 'They were having terrorism problems, just like we do. And he caught 50 terrorists who did tremendous damage and killed many people. And he took the 50 terrorists, and he took 50 men and he dipped 50 bullets in pigs' blood — you heard that, right? He took 50 bullets, and he dipped them in pigs' blood. And he had his men load his rifles, and he lined up the 50 people, and they shot 49 of those people. And the 50th person, he said: You go back to your people, and you tell them what happened. And for 25 years, there wasn't a problem. Okay? Twenty-five years, there wasn't a problem.' See **Reality.**

Geneva Convention: Pussies Who Don't Realize Anything Goes in War. It Ain't Playing Checkers. See **There's No Such Thing As a War Crime in the War on Terror Or the War on the U.S. Media.**

Genocide: If I were president during the Vietnam War, it would have been over fast. See **Nuclear Option.**

Germany: 'A total mess due to the crime caused by allowing migrants into the country.'

Germs: A bigger threat than North Korea, Liberals, Immigrants or Isis. Wash your hands. At least 500 times a day.

Global Warming: 'A hoax perpetuated by the Chinese to get an economic advantage on the U.S.'

Look, Those Silly Americans Think It's True.

Golf: 'Let golf be elitist. Something to aspire to. You work hard, you get to play golf.'

Aspire!

Golf Lessons for Life to Obama:

Following

If Obama resigns from office NOW, thereby doing a great service to the country—I will give him free lifetime golf at any one of my courses!

2:22 PM · 10 Sep 2014

Golf Trophy: 'I dedicate the President Cup's Golf Trophy to the victims of Hurricane Maria.'

Try not to eat it all in one meal.

Goofy: See **Elizabeth Warren**, who also doubles as **Pocahantas.** See **Mitt Romney and George Will**, who also moonlight as **Dopey.**

Greatness: The Donald takes half the property in the world in a tie with Putin in the *Risk* board game. I thoughtfully throw a few crumbs from the top of my tower to my loving base below (well, to those who are still alive, anyway).

Winter is Coming

The Great Unifier: ‘I’m the President of all Americans.’

Greed: It’s what makes the world go ‘round. ‘You can never have enough.’

Grope: It ain’t gropin’ when you know they want it, and they know they want it too. See **Twenty-Four Sexual Assault Complaints.**

H

Hands: 'I have big hands. Rubio has small hands. You know what that means...' See **Master Debater.**

Hard Times: 'I thought being President would be easier than my old life. This is hard. It takes heart. Buying and selling don't take heart.'

Has anyone seen the missing piece?

Hate: The lowest common denominator. See **Steve Bannon**.

Hawaii Official Murdered in Birth Certificate Cover Up: See **Don Quixote Attacking An Innocent Windmill.**

Hero: 'Not John Mccain.' See **Putin.**

Hidden Fee: 1.2 million dollars taken from Eric Trump's Charity Golf Event and added to the Donald's fortune. See **the Really, Really, Small Print.**

Highest Aspiration: Ask not what your country can do for you, but what you can do to play golf. See **Golf.**

Hoax: See **Global Warming**. See the **Russian Investigation.**

How Can A Rich Boy Survive: 'It's reverse discrimination...A well-educated black has a tremendous advantage over a well-educated white in terms of the job market...if I was starting off today, I would love to be a well-educated black, because I really do believe they have the actual advantage today.' See **Sympathy for the Donald.**

Humble: 'I think I'm humble...more humble than anyone understands.' I'm quite proud of my humility, really.

I

Illegal Mexican Immigrants: 'Drug dealers and rapists sent by Mexico to bring us down.'

A poco?

Imaginary Enemies: See **Windmills, Islam.**

Imaginary Events: There are no imaginary events. There are only alternative facts. See **Alternative Facts.**

You say tomato, I say fake news.

Imaginary Friend: See **Trump Publicist John Bannon/John Miller.** See **Putin**. See **Bannon**. See **Harvey the Giant Rabbit below.**

Harvey, the Giant Rabbit

Impeachment: Sour grape Democrats who can't get over losing.

Inaugural Crowd: 'The biggest crowd ever. Of course, the media won't show that.'

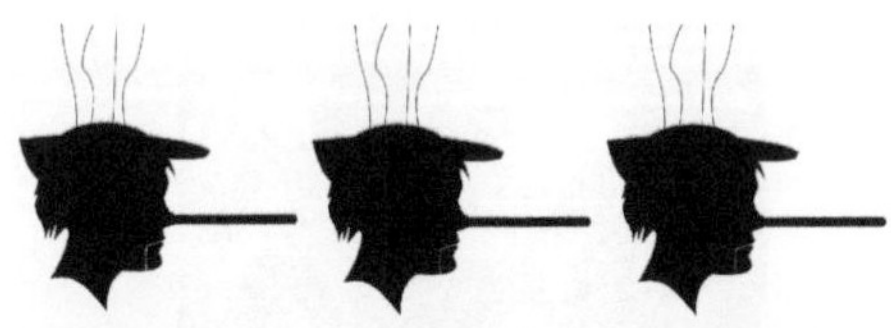

Inauguration: See **The Court Jester Becomes King.**

Intelligence Sharing with Russia Without Permission from Israelis:

You just gave the Russians classified information about a terrorist plot.
'I never mentioned Israel.'
No, you just named the city where it was gathered! Don't you think the Russians can figure out where that is!

See **But I Never Mentioned Israel.**

I.Q.: 'I have one of the highest and everybody knows it. Please don't feel stupid or insecure. It's not your fault.' See **Hands.**

ISIS: 'I know a lot more about ISIS than the generals do. Believe me. Yes, I have a plan to totally destroy Radical Islam Terrorism, but I'm not going to tell you what it is.'

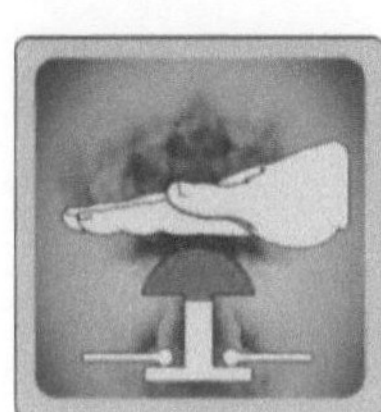

Islam: 'Hates us.' See **Imaginary Enemies.**

Israel: 'I've just come in from the Middle East. Nice to be here in Jerusalem.'

What? You Never Skipped A Class or Two?

It Ain't A Conspiracy If Me and My Fans Believe It's True Even If There Is No Evidence: See Asbestos Is 100 Percent Healthy, Birtherism, Dream of My Father, Exercise Causes You to Die Early, Global Warming is a Hoax, Hawaii Official Murdered in Birth Certificate Cover Up, Barry Soetoro, Columbia University, Obama Will Start A War to Raise His Poll Numbers, Obama Doesn't Want to Fight Terrorism, Obama Wears a Secret Muslim Ring, Obama Aids Terrorists, Obama Is a Muslim, Obama Wiretapping, Scalia Was Murdered, One Hundred Percent of Mosques in America Preach Hate, General Pershing, Vaccines Cause Autism...

Don Quixote Fighting The Good Fight

Ivanka Trump: 'If she weren't my daughter, perhaps I'd be dating her.'

Gross, Dad. Can I use my private email for government communications?

Sure. Why not?

J

James Comey, Former F.B.I Director: 'Nut job! Fired!'

Jeb Bush: To quote my ex-wife, 'No more bush.'

Job Growth: 'Walmart announced it will create 10,000 jobs in the United States just this year because of our various plans and initiatives.'

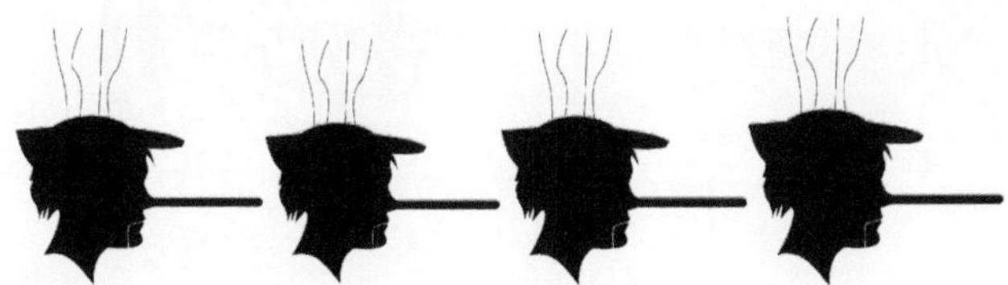

John McCain, Senator from Arizona, Vietnam P.O.W: A fake war hero. 'Heroes don't get caught.'

Judge Gonzalo P. Curiel: 'Totally biased because he's Mexican.' See **Trump University.**

Judicial Branch of the U.S. Government: 'Rigged. In chaos. Not supreme. These so-called judges have no right to review a president's decision about illegal immigration even if they convene constitutional rights and protections. Who do they think they are?'

Roll Over Jefferson! Tell Adams the News!

K

Kate Middleton's Leaked Topless Photos: 'Who wouldn't take Kate's picture and make lots of money as she does the nude sunbathing thing. Come on Kate!'

Kellyanne Conway, Counselor to the President: Sexy, very, very creative. See **7.5**.

Kow-Tow To No One: Except the base. Then screw them hard with Trumpcare and/or Tax Code and blame it on Republicans.

L

Leakers: Grown men and women wetting their pants at the sight of a real man. See **Death Penalty**.

Lies: 1) There are no lies, just alternative facts. 2) Everything the dishonest media says.

Lincoln Tweets and Retweets: See **Presidential.**

Lightweight: See **Loser.**

Little Rocket Man: Me and Little Rocket Man at a urinal trough, measuring each other's arsenal. Guess who wins?

Loser: Anyone who disagrees with the Donald and doesn't have enough money as me. For those who disagree and have money, see **Dumb**.

Love: See **Ratings.**

Lover of Birds: We don't wanna hurt no birds. Not by ugly wind turbines anyway. If they run into my buildings, that's their dumb fault.

Bird 1: The Donald loves us.
Bird 2: Oh yes. I particularly appreciated the condolence letter for Jonathan Livingston Jr. when he flew into the Trump Tower.

Lyin' Ted Cruz: 'Holds the Bible high, then lies and misrepresents the facts...biggest liar in politics...doesn't have the temperament to be president. Are we sure he was born here?'

M

Make America Great Again: One nation devolving together. See **Regression.**

Marco Rubio, Senator from Florida: 'Can you imagine Putin sitting there waiting for a meeting and Rubio walks in and he's totally drenched. I don't know what it is, but I've never seen a human being sweat like this man sweats. Did anyone check his birth certificate?'

Master Debater: They turned on in record numbers just to see me. I mean they were seriously turned on.

I have that effect on women.

Megyn Kelly: 'Overrated lightweight with blood coming out of her eyes and out of her whatever.'

Meryl Streep: 'One of the most over-rated actresses in Hollywood, doesn't know me but attacked last night at the Golden Globes. She is a Hillary flunky who lost big.'

Mexicans Paying for the Wall:

Border Officer: Drug dealer or Rapist?
Pedro: Errrr...neither.
Border Officer: Drugo dealero or rapisto?
Pedro: Still neither.
Border Officer: Border tax, please.
Pedro: Border tax?
Border Officer: Yeah, ten percent goes to my pocket...the rest to the Pay for the Wall fund.
Pedro: Seriously?
Border Officer: As a massive Trump hard-on.
Pedro: Then I'll be legal?
Border Officer: Nah...but we'll still be chasin' your ass...but we'll

give you a good runnin' start and cover one eye when we shoot.
Pedro: Will you take 100 pesos?
Border Officer: It's gonna take more than that if you want to get past that wall.
Pedro: 100 pesos and a donkey?
Border Officer: Son, if you don't come up with 5,000 dollars, we're gonna have to lock you up.
Pedro: Ah....Jeez...I already paid on the Mexican side.

Mucho Wallo, Poco Dinero

Mika Brzezinski, Member of the Enemy Press: 'Bleeding badly from bad face lift. Dumb as a rock.'

Miss Universe: Huge success and they all want The Donald. See **Hands.**

Mitch McConnell, Senate Majority Leader: What have you guys been doing the last seven years?

Money: See **Ratings.**

The Most Interesting Man in the World: I don't drink beer often, but when I do, it ain't Mexican.

Musical Chairs: See **There is No Chaos in the Cabinet. Everything Is Fine.**

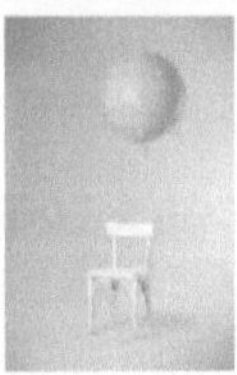

Muslims: 'They're hard to tell from terrorists.'

My African-American: 'You're my African American.' See **The Only African-American Supporter at Trump Rally.**

N

Nambia: You can get rich there, my fellow covfefe. Just enroll in my Trump University and I'll show you how. A special discount for my loyal base...Oh, wait, I forgot...that racist Mexican Judge shut us down.

You Don't Have to Know How to Spell It To Make Money There

NAFTA: 'The worst deal ever. We have a multimillion dollar deficit with Canada.' See **Alternative Facts.**

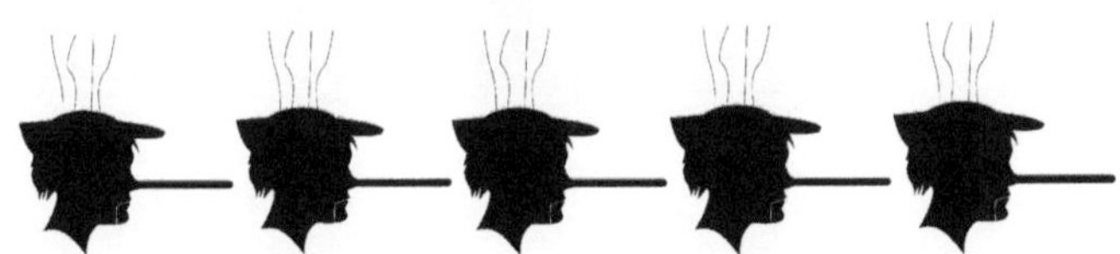

Na-Na-Na-Na: I can say Radical Islamic Terrorism.

Get Ready for This Golf Ball, Hillary!

Narcissism: If loving me is wrong, I don't wanna be right.

NATO: 'Obsolete because it doesn't cover terrorism.'

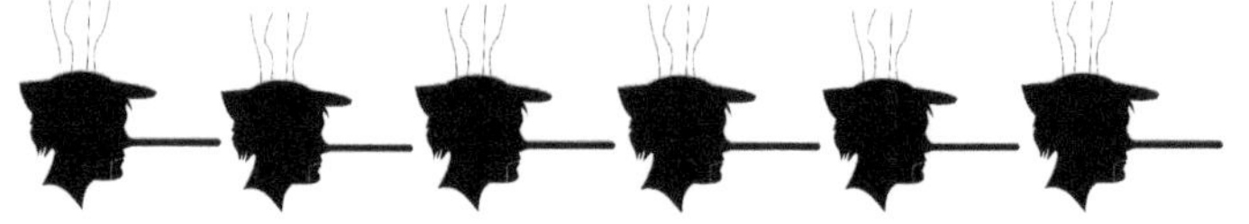

Neil Young: 'Hypocrite.' A Southern Man doesn't need him around anyway. Or a Northern Man. Or any Real Man.

Nepotism: It's my business, and I'll run it as I see fit. It's not like you professional politicians are doing any better. 'And so what if Ivanka sits in for me at the G20 Summit. Very standard. If Hillary had done the same with Chelsea, the enemy of a press would've praised her.'

Good morning Mr. President. It would never have occurred to my mother or my father to ask me. Were you giving our country away? Hoping not.

Donald J. Trump @realDonaldTrump
If Chelsea Clinton were asked to hold the seat for her mother,as her mother gave our country away, the Fake News would say CHELSEA FOR PRES!

The New York Times: 'Writers of fake news, haters, failin'. They don't write good.'

NFL Owners Who Support the Player Protesters: 'Afraid of their own players.'

NFL Player Protesters: 'Sons a bitches who need to be fired. If the NFL doesn't change, its ratings will go to hell.'

Hellfire to Sons a bitches!

Nipplephobia: Don't breastfeed in public if over 40. Don't be seen in public without a bra if you're Barney Frank.

North Korean Diplomacy Talks: 'Stop it, Rex. You can't reason with Little Rocket Man. We'll do what we need to do.'

Nuclear Option: Smoke 'em if you got 'em. 'Why can't we? 'Why can't we? Why can't we?'

I asked you three times. Your lack of an answer and wide open mouth must mean that you are dazzled by superior intelligence.

O

Obamacare:

Me: Bad. Very very very bad.
Dishonest Reporter: Have you read it?
Me: No...but it's bad...very very very bad.
Dishonest Reporter: How do you know?
Me: I don't have to read that disaster. Obama did it, right?

Obama's Secret Muslim Ring: It says 'There is No God but Allah. Who does this guy think he is?' See **Don Quixote Declaring Victory!**

Obama Wiretapping of Trump Tower: Who needs evidence when you can feel it in your groin area?

Mr. President, are you wearing a wire in your scrotum area?

One Hundred Percent of Mosques in America Preach Hate: 'If you look at the mosques and you go to various places and you look at what's going on there and it's virtually 100 percent hatred. I think Islam hates us.' See **Never Underestimate The Power of Paranoia and Fear Mongering in Building A Loyal Base.**

Orange: Second Favorite color.

It ain't orange. It's blonde, stupid.

Orwell: Some no-talent, overrated loser who wrote a book in 1984.

P

Paranoia: 'The Mayor of San Juan, who was very complimentary only a few days ago, has now been told by the Democrats that you must be nasty to Trump.' See **Attack of the Disney Characters: Dopey, Goofy, Dumbo and Pocahantas.**

It Ain't Paranoia If You're Really Seeing Things in The Dark

Paris Climate Accord: Let the rest of the world take care of those photoshopped pictures of hot Polar bears. I'm the President of

Pittsburgh. Not Paris. And if we need to emit a little gas, we certainly will.

I wished for a sauna. Who knew it would come true?

Patriotism: Don't blindly follow your incompetent government, just your president.

I Want You, Especially If You're a Blonde 10

Paul Ryan, Speaker of the House: 'Weak, ineffectual.'

Phalacrophobia: Fear of going bald.

Mr. President, your hair is trying to leave the building. The Secret Service is way over budget. We can't defend you and your hair.

Pocahantas: See **Elizabeth Warren.**

Police Brutality: Animals don't deserve rights. 'Don't be too nice.'

Political Correctness: 'It's killin' our country.' Since when can't you call a spade a spade, an NFL player a son-of-a-bitch, a fat woman a pig, an LGBT or a breastfeeder in public disgusting.

Political Incorrectness: Taking back our country, one word at time. See **Anthony Scaramucci.** See **Your President in Action Everyday.**

Political Science: Listen to Randy Newman's great Patriotic song, *Political Science (Let's Drop the Big One Now).*

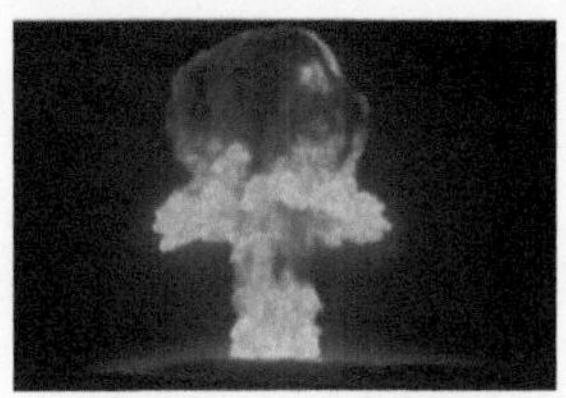

Polls: Lies told by the liberal media enemy--except when they're in the Donald's favor.

Popularity: 'I'm so popular I could shoot someday in the middle of the day and still not go down in the polls.'

Popular Vote: 'Between 3 and 5 million illegal votes caused me to lose the Popular Vote.'

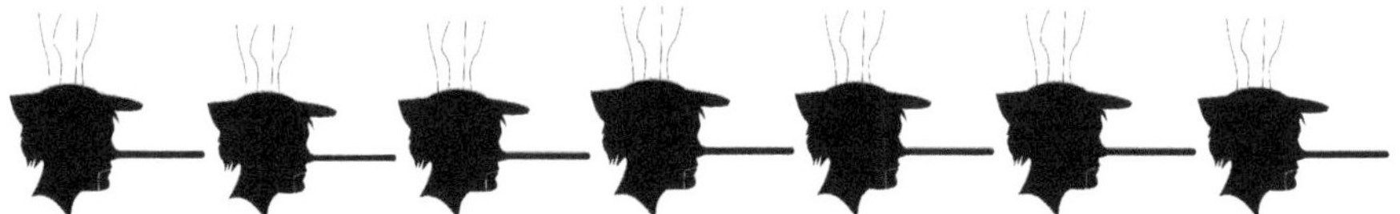

Power: See **Ratings.**

The Presidency: See **Reality TV show.**

Presidential: Lincoln and me, except Lincoln didn't have Twitter.

Lincoln Tweets?

Processed Food: 'Always eat food that is standardized. That way you always know where it's coming from.' See **Germs.**

Protesters: Losers and thugs hired by rich Liberals.

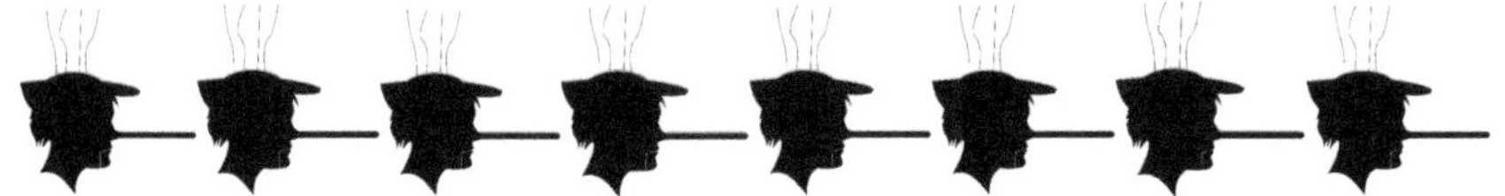

Psychiatry: 'Who needs psychiatry when you have Twitter?' See **Bullying**.

Puerto Ricans: 'They want everything to be done for them.' See **Racist.**

Mr. President, Can You Pass the Sun Screen?

Puerto Rico Natural Disaster: Who knew they were citizens? A devastating distraction from my feud with the NFL.

Purpose of Life: Get rich and have others adore you. Fire those who don't get it. If you can't fire 'em, bully them.

Putin:

Sept. 13, 2013

'You think of the term *American Exceptionalism* as being fine, but all of sudden you say, what if you're in Germany or Japan or any one of 100 different countries? You're not going to like that term. It's very insulting and Putin really put it to him (Obama) about that.'

April 12, 2014

'Putin could not have been nicer. He was so nice and so everything. But you have to give him credit that what he's doing for that country in terms of their world prestige is very strong...Well, he's done an amazing job of taking the mantle. And so smart. When you see the riots in a country because they're hurting the Russians, OK, 'We'll go and take it over.' And he really goes step by step by step, and you have to give him a lot of credit.'

Beautiful, isn't It?

It's not bad, but I prefer red sunsets.

Dec. 30, 2015, South Carolina Rally

'Putin says I'm brilliant. My opponents want me to refute his statement.' See **Hero.**

Trumputin. Get on the train.

Q

The Quality of Character: Who needs it when you have gobs of money?

The Quality of Money

R

Racist: 'I'm the least racist person.'
See **'I'm Not A Crook, I Don't Even Know What a Crook Is, Nixon.** See **Read My Lips, No New Taxes, Bush 1.** See **I Didn't Put It In, I Only Stained Her Dress, Clinton.**

Radical Islamic Terrorism: Radical Islamic Terrorism. Radical Islamic Terrorism Radical Islamic Terrorism. Radical Islamic Terrorism. Radical Islamic Terrorism. Na na na na. I can say it. Obama couldn't even say it. How can you fight it if you can't even say it? See **Political Correctness**.

Rand Paul: 'A spoiled brat without a properly functioning brain.'

Rand Paul: That's not true! I have a perfectly normal brain. Sounds like you are describing yourself!

The Donald: No way! I'm not a spoiled brat!

Ratings: See **Love, Money and Power.**

Reading: Anything over 140 characters I have no attention for. That's why I have staff.

Why Isn't the Senate Intel Committee looking into the Fake News Networks in OUR country to see why so much of our news is just made up-FAKE!

3:59 AM · 5 Oct 2017

Reality: What I say it is. See **Truth.**

Reality Check: 'Was it over when the Germans bombed Pearl Harbor,' Bluto Blutarsky from *Animal House*. 'The Germans?' 'Forget it, he's rollin'...'

Reality TV Show: See **The Presidency.**

Recurring Nightmare 1: I wake up bald.

Recurring Nightmare 2: I wake up with Rosie O' Donnell.

Recurring Nightmare 3: I wake up with blood in my sheets and the horse mouth of Megyn Kelly. See **The Godfather.**

Recurring Nightmare 4: They've found my taxes.

Recurring Nightmare 5: I wake up with Lyin' Ted Cruz's wife.

Recurring Nightmare 6: I'm having dinner in the White house dump of a kitchen.

Recurring Nightmare 7: Hannibal Lechter is the chef.

Your dinner is ready, Mr. President
What is it?
It's your brain, Mr. President. Try it. It's good for you.
My brain?
Yes, Secret Service found it. Perhaps you misplaced it?

Recurring Nightmare 8: The Tin Man from *Wizard of Oz* is a heart salesmen.

We have several fine hearts to choose from, Mr. President.
What's that?
It's the muscle in most chests that pumps blood...
I already have a heart! Get out of here!

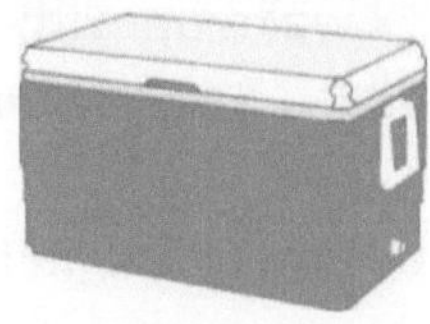

Recurring Nightmare 9: I wake up shivering. Putin's taken all the bedsheets.

Recurring Nightmare 10: I'm being attacked by Disney Characters. Dumbo the Republican Establishment is sitting on me. I can't breathe. Goofy's slapping my right cheek. I turn the other one. Dopey slaps it. Pocahantas scalps me, takes my hair.

Recurring Nightmare 11: General Kelly is waterboarding me. He's pouring water over a cloth over my face.

General: Do you think it's good idea to undermine your Secretary of State with your stupid tweets while he's attempting diplomacy with the North Koreans in your name! (He stops to let me speak)

Me: Yes!

General (Continues with the cloth and water): What? (stops)

Me: I mean no.

General: Are you sure?

Me: No, no, no!

General (starts again): What? (stops)

Me: Yes, I mean yes!

General: Good, will you stop?

Me: Yes.

General: Do you think it's a good idea to tease the American public about a possibly military action?

Me: Yes.

General: Here's your calm before the storm! You're 'You'll See!' Do you think the presidency is a reality tv show?

Me: No, no, no....I won't do it again.

General: Good.

Me: But the whole world is a reality show. And I'm the KIng!

General: What? You think you're some kind of king, do you? More like the Court Jester you mean. Only that's an insult to court jesters, who wisely counseled their kings through playful humor. Which are you, Mr. President?

Me: A King with a sense of humor sir. Did you see how the stupid media were so baffled by my tease? Ha ha ha.

General: What? You are the president of the United States. How does a president act?

Me: Like me...

General: I give up. Looks like you need a real court jester...maybe he can help. Robin!

The ghost of Robin Williams enters in full court jester garb.

Robin: *Reality! What a concept!* Reality according to Donald! What a brain fart! *The Statue of Liberty is no longer saying, 'Give me your poor, your tired, your huddled masses.' She's got a baseball bat and yelling, 'You want a piece of me?*

Me: That's good.

Robin: No, no...that's not good. And certainly not great. Mr. President, *your golf bag doesn't contain a full set of irons.*

Me: What? Best irons money can buy.

Robin: Shhh...You conjured me from a nice nap with several angels and you will listen! When I said, *'You're only given a little spark of madness. You mustn't lose it.* I wasn't talking to you who have tiki torches full of it!

Me: Huh?

Robin: Lose it now...at least some of it. Listen. *Change is not popular; we are creatures of habit as human beings. 'I want it to be the way it was.' But if you continue the way it was there will be no 'is.'* Global Warming is real! The flames of Hell are getting closer to Heaven each day. I went to ask the angels about getting a/c and they started an investigation into my membership credentials!

Me: Really?

Robin: What's this with you and asking people to stand for the flag out of respect for the soldiers? That's like Hitler saying, 'More Matzo balls, please.'

Me: What? No...

Robin: Listen! *There's three things in this world that you need: Respect for all kinds of life, a nice bowel movement on a regular basis, and a navy blazer.*

Navy blazer? Check. Nice bowel movement on a regular basis. Every day on Twitter. Check.

Respect for all kinds of life--and not just birds that run into ugly wind turbines near your gold course.

White men who agree with you? Check.
White women? Hmmmm.
Muslims? Hmmmmmm.
What if they were to pray 5 times a day in the direction of the Donald, would that change your mind?

Me: That'd be great.

Robin: No, it wouldn't. That would be stupid. Mexicans? Hmmm. *Come on now! You kick out the spicks, the next thing you know, you have to kick out the chinks, the gooks, the spooks, the kikes and all that's going to be left is a couple of brain-dead rednecks.*

Religion: See **Evangelicals.** See **Greed.**

Repeal of Obama's Gun Restriction on the Mentally Ill: Crazy people need guns too.

Republicans: 'Dishonest, failing, disloyal people out for themselves. Can't even pass Healthcare.' They are the elephant in the room!

Right-Wing Racists: Good people. See **Base.**

Rigged: Any system or process that doesn't have the outcome the Donald wants.

Rosie O' Donnell: 'A fat pig. I feel sorry for Rosie 's new partner in love whose parents are devastated at the thought of their daughter being with Rosie--a true loser.'

Roy Moore, Alabama Republican: Anyone who pulls out a gun at his own campaign rally can't be all bad, right?

Russians: Very helpful come election time. I got friends in far places.

S

Sancho Panza: Italian for Sean Hannity; Don Quixote's sidekick.

Satire: What's that? See **Political Science.**

The Second Amendment: Guarantees the right to bear arms. Give all Americans guns. No more mass killings.

Science: Who needs it when superstition and common sense do just fine. See **Asbestos.** See **Global Warming.**

Sean Hannity: A great American. Loyal as a Collie. If the entire press were like him, I'd be on a par with Putin.

Fighting the Good Fight with the Donald Quixote

Sean Spicer: Bad suits and played by a woman. Weak. 'But good ratings. He'll do fine.'

Self-Awareness: Who needs it when you have Self-Belief?

Seven-Year-Mitch: See **Mitch McConnell**.

Sexism: A fake term created by a woman as an excuse not to wear heels or make up or go on a diet.

Sex Objects: Women. Me.

Sheriff Joe Arpaio: 'A great American Patriot.' If you were brown you knew Sheriff Joe was in town. And when the dopey judge ordered him to stop detaining people just because he suspected them of being illegal, he refused to go to the back of the bus! A great man worthy of pardon!

Stop in the Name of Xenophobia!

Sleep Deprivation: I only get a few hours sleep every night. And then it's time to tweet. Real men don't need sleep. See **Covfefe**.

Son-of-a-Bitch: See **Political Incorrectness.** See **NFL Players.**

Star Power: 'You know, I'm automatically attracted to beautiful — I just start kissing them. It's like a magnet. Just kiss. I don't even wait. And when you're a star, they let you do it. You can do anything....Grab them by the pussy. You can do anything.' See **Rich Privileges.**

The State of Politics: 'One of they key problems today is that politics is such a disgrace. Good people don't go into government.'

Steve Bannon: Editor of *Breitbart,* former adviser to Trump, smart man. See **Alt-Right.** See **Genius.**

Stubborn: A sign of greatness. Great men never give in.

Swedish Terrorist Attack: More proof we need extensive Travel Ban on Muslims and Swedes!

Chelsea Clinton
@ChelseaClinton
Following

What happened in Sweden Friday night? Did they catch the Bowling Green Massacre perpetrators?

4:50 AM - 19 Feb 2017

40,386 Retweets **116,735** Likes

See **Imaginary Events.**

Sympathy for the Donald: Allow me to introduce myself, I'm a man of wealth and wealth.

T

Tax Records: I'll show you mine if you show me yours.

Thin Skin: See **Tough.** Don't See **I Fall to Pieces if Anyone Criticizes Me.**

Only overrated losers would see that

Thousands Of Muslim-Americans In New Jersey Celebrated On 9/11 'I believe it happened and there's footage somewhere, but it's not politically correct for the Fake News Media to show it.' See **Your Mama's A Conspiracy Theory, Moron.**

There they are! Look!

Tips from Ex-Wife on How to Handle the Donald If You Are A Puerto Rican Citizen Who Desperately Needs Food, Water and Power:

1) Bow.
2) Kiss the Ring
3) Show a little cleavage.
4) Wear a Blonde wig, if possible.
5) Tell him how fit he looks.
6) Tell him how great he is.
7) Tell him how smart is.
8) Tell him how stupid the Media Is.
9) Tell him how great a job he is doing.
10) Ask politely for help.

Tip from Ex-Wife to Military Advisers: Try Reverse Psychology. See **Dustin Hoffman in *Little Big Man* Advising Custer on What Would Be His Last Stand: 'You Go Down There General If You Got the Nerve.'**

Torture and Murder: 'The most efficient way to stop terrorism. That and killing the families of the terrorists.'

Tough: Real men and great countries must be tough at all times.

Travel Ban: Keeping as many Muslims out of the country as possible no matter what a stupid judge might say about its constitutionality.

Trump First: White Rich America Second.

Trump Publicist John Bannon/John Miller: What? You've never pretended to be someone else?

Trump Tantrum: 'How come every time I show anger, disgust or impatience, enemies say I had a tantrum or meltdown—stupid or dishonest people?'

Because I'm Your President, you Clown!

Trump University: Is it my fault people are gullible? They knew what they were getting into. The right to mingle with and learn with the Donald. Or just to get close to the magic. The court system is rigged. See **Judge Gonzalo P. Curiel.** I paid the 25 million settlement anyway. It's pennies to me.

I got a 2007 Ford Bronco. Great Shape. Great Deal.

Trump Simplifed Tax Code: The rich get richer, the poor get poorer

Trump Values: Selfishness, Greed, Combativeness, Superficiality, Tenacity, Xenophobia.

Twenty-Four Sexual Assault Claims: See **Grope.**

Twitter: 'Modern Day Presidential.' Entertaining the base.

Barney Frank looked disgusting--nipples protruding--in his blue shirt before Congre
Very very disrespectful.

12:36 PM · 21 Dec 2011

U

United States Intelligence Services: 'Nazis!'

Intelligence agencies should never have allowed this fake news to "leak" into the public. One last shot at me.Are we living in Nazi Germany?

4:48 AM · 11 Jan 2017

Unpatriotic: Those morons who oppose me. Love it or leave it, low-lifes!

V

Vaccines Cause Autism: See **Science.**

Vetting: 'We've taken in tens of thousands of people. We know nothing about them. They can say they vet them. They didn't vet them. They have no papers. How can you vet somebody when you don't know anything about them and you have no papers? How do you vet them? You can't.' See **The More Extreme the Vetting, the Better.**

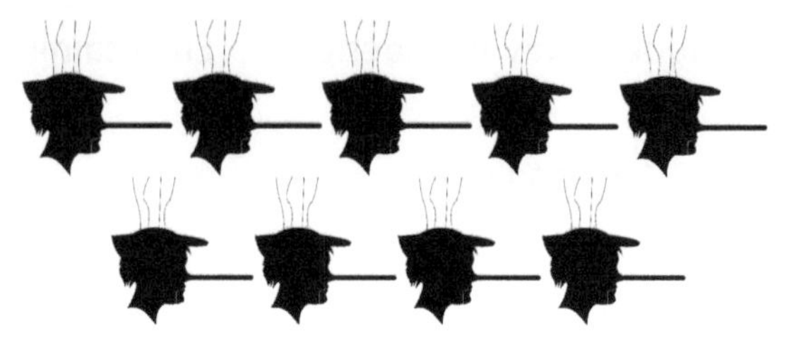

W

The Wall: I'll keep them Mexicans out if it's the last thing I do.

The Walton School, University of Pennsylvania: Best diploma money can buy. See **Brains, baby, brains.**

Weakness: Real men don't have weakness.

White Finnish Reporters:

Me: 'She just asked a question.'
Finnish President: 'That's not the same reporter.'

See **White People All Look Alike**.

The White House: 'A real dump.'

Wild Bill: 'Bill Clinton.'

Windmills: 'They spoil the view of my golf course...kill millions of birds.' See **Ariana Huffington Without Makeup.** See **Barney Frank Without a Bra.** See **Go Quixote, Go!**

Winter Weather: 'It's freezing and snowing in New York. We could use some Global Warming.'

Witch Hunt: Citizen posse in search of Megyn Kelly; Russian Investigation. See **Comey and Mueller.**

Women: Go well with a ten thousand dollar suit; good for groping 'cause you know they want it...Who can resist the Donald? See **Accessories.**

Words I Have Trouble Saying Together: KKK, Evil.

Worst Job in the World: White House Press Secretary. See **Tough.**

X

Xenophobia: Latin for *Law of the Land.*

Photo Credits

Blonde Female Reporter, CNN screenshot
Bowling Green Massacre, Twitter screenshot/Chelsea Clinton
Brigitte Macron, CNN screenshot
Bullying, Twitter screenshot/Donald Trump
Crooked Hillary, Twitter screenshot/Donald Trump
Disabled Reporter, Twitter/CNN screenshot
Eclipse, WH screenshot
Fake News, Twitter screenshot/Donald Trump
Golf Lessons for Life for Obama, Twitter screenshot/Donald Trump
Nepotism, Twitter screenshot/Chelsea Clinton
Phalacrophobia, Twitter screenshot
Presidential, Twitter screenshot/New York Post
Reading, Twitter screenshot /Donald Trump
Twitter, Twitter screenshot/Donald Trump
United States Intelligence Services, Twitter screenshot/Donald Trump
White Finnish Reporters, Twitter screenshot/CNN

Photos Used Under the Fair Use Doctrine.

All Other Photos are from the Artists at Pixabay/Thanks!

Used by Permission:

CCO Creative Commons
Free for commercial use
No attribution required

Other Credits

Recurring Dream 11:

Words in *italics* are direct quotes from Robin Williams, whom we sorely miss.

Website

http://raysweatman.com

Special Thanks to Ambrose Bierce for the inspiration.